IMAGES
of America

RURAL YORK
COUNTY

IMAGES
of America

RURAL YORK COUNTY

Compiled by
Allan Swenson, Boyd Swenson, and Kathy Fink

ARCADIA

ISBN 0 7524 0089 4

Published by Arcadia Publishing,
an imprint of the Chalford Publishing Corporation
One Washington Center, Dover , New Hampshire 03820
Printed in Great Britain

Library of Congress Cataloging-in-Publication Data applied for

Contents

Introduction

Rural York County, with its charming, historic towns and villages, has long been one of the most delightful areas of Maine and New England. As early as the beginning of the nineteenth century, southern Maine was seen by both residents and visitors as an area of beauty and friendliness.

Too often, writers have focused on the seacoast and the larger cities of York County. That is probably fortunate for those living in the smaller villages and towns. Reading about the other areas, tourists have been attracted elsewhere, especially along the rocky coast of Maine. Happily, that has allowed the rural areas to enjoy the security, peace, and proud sense of identity provided by quiet country living.

The roots of the towns that make up rural York County extend deeply into the past. For the first century of settlement in New England all but the coast of York County was populated and controlled by Native Americans. However, by the mid-nineteenth century the burgeoning population of the Massachusetts Bay Colony changed matters. Seeking an outer ring of defense against the Native Americans the Massachusetts General Court gave land grants to areas running in an arc from North Berwick to Buxton, Windham, and New Gloucester. In turn this arc allowed more settlers to pour into what is now northern York County—Limerick, Newfield, Parsonsfield, Cornish, and Limington. The rivers, the Saco and Ossipee in particular, provided the major routes of travel. Thus the area was settled and generations of families tilled the soil, tended their crops and livestock, and raised their families.

We began this book with one idea uppermost in our mind—to look back and remember a gentler time, a time of barn raisings and crop gathering, of community dances and buckboard rides to church and one-room schoolhouses. This selection represents many hours of poring through photograph albums and books in an attempt to recapture and convey a sense of "the way things used to be." Readers may remember people and places from the near and distant past, but we also hope you may learn new and fascinating facts as you travel back into the "Good Ol' Days" We have organized the images as a journey from Kittery up the coast to Saco; through the Berwicks and Lebanon; to the county seat at Alfred, and Sanford and Springvale close by; around Acton, Shapleigh, Newfield, and Waterboro; then to Parsonsfield, Porter, Kezar Falls, and Cornish.

These towns possess many different characteristics which make each of them unique, but they also share common traits which make their inhabitants proud to be residents of rural York County, and which keep visitors coming back to this beautiful part of Maine to get a taste of the quieter, perhaps better, life. We hope you enjoy the journey!

Allan Swenson, Boyd Swenson, and Kathy Fink
January 1995

One

From Kittery to Saco

Sir William Pepperrell House, Built 1733, Kittery Point, Maine.

The Sir William Pepperell House at Kittery Point. Built in 1773, this house was a favorite tourist spot for many years.

An appealing early rural scene of the York River as it appeared to visitors and to patients looking over it from the York Hospital. Much of York was settled by Scottish immigrants, some of whom were shipped to New England by Oliver Cromwell as prisoners of war during the English Civil War.

The Old York Jail, built in 1653, is still standing today, and is currently used as a museum. Its rough look speaks of a sterner system of justice in days gone by.

This postcard of the old stone bridge in Cape Neddick was a popular one for tourists to send in the 1900s. The Cape Neddick and York Beach area was one of the most famous tourist areas for wealthy New Yorkers and Bostonians in the late nineteenth century. With the spread of the streetcar system and then the invention of the automobile, tourists visited in ever-increasing numbers and local businesses responded by printing postcards such as this one for visitors to send home.

The Wells Potato Chip Company on Route 1 in Wells was a prosperous early Maine potato business, drawing its supplies from nearby farms.

The famous artist, Abbott Graves, in the garden of his home in Kennebunkport. His paintings were treasured by several generations of art collectors.

Booth Tarkington, one of Maine's more famous authors, lived and wrote many of his novels at his summer home, Seawood Cottage, in Kennebunkport. During the summer he entertained various members of the Algonquin Round Table (a literary group). Today the house has been divided into condominiums.

The Marland Estate as seen from Stone Haven Hill in Cape Porpoise.

A *c.* 1900s photograph of the 1764 Cleaves House at Wildes District in Cape Porpoise. Many families settled in Cape Porpoise in the early part of the eighteenth century.

The famed Lafayette Elm in Kennebunk had a girth of 17 feet 3 inches and stood 131 feet tall. Legend has it that the tree earned its name when General Marquis de Lafayette gave a speech under its giant branches. Today, a boulder marks the spot, which is now a minipark.

The Storer Mansion in Kennebunk, when the old elm still grew through the roof of the barn. This famous and historic home was restored to its former grandeur in 1994.

Members of the Day family gather for a celebration and family portrait. (Nancy Hooper)

Visitors were often treated to pastoral scenes such as this one during their stay. This photograph shows haying in progress at Willow Lane Farm in the 1930s.

Milking time at Willow Lane Farm.

Making silage in the 1930s at Russell's Acres Farm in the Alewive section of Kennebunk was a family chore. In this 1930s photograph, Mr. and Mrs. Russell work to gather winter feed for their cows: Mr. Russell is driving the tractor while Mrs. Russell drives the truck.

Long a prosperous dairy farm, Carl Russell shows visitors some of his top milk-producing cows in the 1950s.

Enjoying a break from farm chores at the original Russell's Acres farmstead. Today, Louise Russell, daughter Carol, and son-in-law Phil Parker operate this delightful farm, which now features deer farming. Louise Russell is famous for her culinary talent.

"Aunt Lill's" guests and staff at Maple Top Farm, Kennebunk, in 1940. Many farms in rural areas earned extra income by taking in summer boarders from as far away as New York and Philadelhphia. These early tourists saw rural York County as a peaceful "getaway" from the bustle of city life.

As modern cars made transportation easier, the Maine countryside and its down-to-earth, friendly inhabitants became increasingly popular as a summer retreat to beat city heat. From their base at these quiet countryside farms, visitors would take day trips to see the sights of coastal Maine.

Main Street looking south from Eastman Park in Saco when early autos shared the road with trolley tracks and trolleys. At the height of the trolley system in York County it was all but possible to ride trolleys from Kittery to Portland.

Monument Square in Saco, when horses and wagons brought farm families from north Saco, Buxton, and Dayton to town to sell their farm produce and shop.

Two

The Berwicks and Lebanon

South Berwick's Maine Street in early 1900s. Visiting today, you'll see many of these same buildings.

Volunteers gather at the old sawmill pond in South Berwick in 1865 to practice their fire-fighting skills.

Knights Pond in South Berwick was a popular summer retreat for Mainers and early visitors alike.

A view of the post office in Berwick in the days of the horse and buggy.

Postmen, with their horses and buggies ready to go, prepare to deliver the day's mail. This is the Berwick Post Office as it looked c. 1907.

The Nutes House in Berwick at the turn of the century.

Dressed in their Sunday Best, a couple prepares for a drive to town in the Sunday carriage.

Posing for postcard photographs was a special treat before cameras became a common household possession.

Main Street in North Berwick showing the passing of an era as horseless carriages share the street with horses and buggies.

S. Buffum's box mill, one of the successful early businesses in North Berwick.

A lake shore cottage at Bauneg-Beg Lake in North Berwick about 1917. The lake remains a popular summer home area for many Mainers.

A crew of workmen pause for a picture at the H.J. Henderson saw mill in Lebanon , *c.* 1908. Lebanon was originally the plantation of Towwoh, and was incorporated in 1767.

The Lebanon grist mill at Little River Falls, 1911.

Ice houses as they appeared in Lebanon in 1911.

Eastwood Railroad Station in Lebanon in the early *1900s*.

Eastwood Station in Lebanon *c*. 1910. Note the new building on the right of the tracks.

The Congregational Meeting House in Center Lebanon in 1908.

Pine Spring Farm,
Lebanon, Maine,

Pine Spring Farm in Lebanon was a pleasant spot for vacationers in 1908.

Two people enjoy a boat outing next to the railroad bridge on the Salmon Falls River in 1908. This portion of Lebanon has as much in common with New Hampshire, its western border, as with Maine.

Northeast Pond in Lebanon was a popular boating pond in the 1930s.

The Hillside School of West Lebanon 1908. It became the Sundal Guest House in the 1930s.

The Sundal Guest House parlor as decorated in 1930s.

In the early part of the century photographers would travel the countryside to take family portraits such as this one. This is the Murray family at their farm in Lebanon in 1909. They have obviously dressed up for the occasion.

A side view of Seven Elms in West Lebanon, showing a wonderful screened veranda, *c.* 1927.

A family gathers on a veranda at one of the summer boarding retreats in West Lebanon around 1915. Doesn't it look peaceful?

The Ole Bull residence in West Lebanon in 1940s. It was the home of the Shapleigh family in the mid-1880s; and in the late 1800s it became the residence of "Ole Bull," a well-known concert violinist.

Bonnie View Farm in West Lebanon c. 1908. The farm was a popular boarding place for summer visitors in the early 1900s.

A 1908 photograph, looking northeast, of two churches on the main road through West Lebanon.

The Free Baptist Church in West Lebanon, c. 1915.

The Academy Building in West Lebanon as it appeared in 1909.

The West Lebanon Post Office in 1915 with Postmaster Cowell leaning in the doorway.

A 1908 photogrpah of the schoolhouse in East Lebanon.

The Little River Baseball Club of East Lebanon posing for a team picture in 1909. Baseball was very different back then, but the players looked pretty much the same as today's young players.

The T.R. Wentworth store in East Lebanon as it appeared in 1908.

1060. E.J. GERRISH FARM
EAST LEBANON, ME.

The E.J. Gerrish Farm in East Lebanon in 1911.

The early twentieth century, before the invention and widespread use of the telephone, was the heyday of the postcard. Postcard photographers and printers would create postcards of even the tiniest communities to be used as a quick and easy method of communication. Luckily for historians, many of these postcards have survived as important historical documents. These postcards were taken in North Lebanon in 1911 and show the post office and store (top), and the square (bottom).

North Lebanon village as it appeared in 1908.

The home of Fred Hanscom at Hanscom's Corner in North Lebanon was popular for its community water pump on the front lawn.

A 1908 photograph of the Freewill Baptist Church in North Lebanon.

The Free Baptist Parsonage in North Lebanon was the birthplace of Congressman Charles E. Littlefield.

Three
Alfred, Sanford, and Springvale

The Alfred Common, when gravel roads led people into town. Alfred is the exact physical center of York County, and is the county seat. The choice of Alfred over Kennebunk as the shiretown in the 1800s apparently involved questionable vote-counting.

York County Courthouse in Alfred was the center for legal matters in this shiretown when York County was still rural. It is noted for having some of the oldest continuing land records and deeds in the United States.

The York County Jail, depicted in a postcard dated 1903, is described by the sender as his "boarding house" during his visit to Maine.

Parson's Memorial Library in Alfred as it looked in 1906. It retains that same classic look today, even with additions to it.

Alfred House in Alfred, shown here c. 1906, was a vacation retreat for city folks in the good old days.

lfred, Maine., View of Railroad.

A postcard of a steam locomotive puffing its way through Alfred.

Pastoral scenes of the Sanford countryside made popular postcards in the early 1900s.

Main Street in Sanford in the 1930s.

Lower Main Street in Sanford in the 1930s, as seen from the windows of the Sanford Hotel.

The residences of F.J. Allen, George B. Goodall, and L.B. Goodall on Lower Main Street in the 1930s. The Goodall mills were the largest employers in Sanford until they moved south after World War II.

The Leavitt Block in Sanford in the early 1930s.

A more modern photograph of the Leavitt Block, which is still standing at the corner of Washington and School Streets.

A view of School Street, Sanford, before the roads were paved.

A *c.* 1930s view of School Street from the post office.

50

An early 1900s photograph of the Philpot home on the corner of Lebanon and Nason Streets in Sanford. As late as the 1970s this lovely old house was still being used for apartment dwellings, but it was torn down in 1979.

The Hotel Sanford, as shown on a postcard mailed in 1912.

The McDougal house in Sanford ready for winter occupancy in 1924.

Two lovely photographs of the McDougal children taken in 1926. On the left is Robert McDougal out skiing, and on the right the children play "dress up."

The McDougal children on the running board of the family car in Springvale in 1928.

A McDougal family outing at
Drakes Island, Wells, in 1938.

The Boston and Maine Railroad station in Sanford and Springvale. Note the horses and wagons near at hand and the trolley about to depart.

Trains were an important mode of transportation in Sanford and Springvale in the early years of this century.

This Gerrish family portrait was taken in 1906.

The Gerrish family in 1930.

Hiram N. Gerrish receives a medal from Charles Goodwin in 1937 for walking across the country to visit three of his children in California. The trip took four years and he often became the guest of Indian tribes along the way.

Springvale is the northwestern portion of Sanford. A rural section of the town, Springvale was home to Nasson College for much of the century. Sadly, the school closed some fifteen years ago.

A winter view of Butler Square in Springvale, *c.* 1909.

Two men stand near a horse-drawn cart in front of L.B. Stiles Boot, Shoe, and Clothing store. This building was destroyed by fire in July 1881.

Butchers went from door to door in the early part of the century. Here, Leander Smith is standing beside his horse-drawn cart in Springvale.

A horse and two men can hardly find room near the hitching post of a building during the great blizzard of March 12, 1888.

A cart being pulled by oxen in front of Dennett's Store in May 1897. Greeting each other are John Dennett and Al Goodwin, as a third gentleman looks on.

Three gentlemen pose inside the L.B. Trafton Drugstore in the Butler Block of Springvale Square in 1909. Note the metal ceiling and glass cases of the day, as well as the soda fountain stool in the foreground.

The Springvale Fire Department in the early 1900s.

A 1920s photograph of the Hanson farmhouse in Springvale.

The Springvale Public Library seen has changed remarkably little over the years.

The front of the Springvale Public Library.

The Angie Shuckley house in the early 1900s.

The home of Mrs. I.C. Sawyers later became the main hall of the Nasson Institute.

The Nasson Institute as it looked in the early 1900s. Originally, the Nasson Institute educated women in home economics. Later it became a four-year private college with an experimental section similar to Goddard College in Vermont.

Makins Field was a popular place for athletic meets. In this 1909 photograph, a May Day event is taking place on the site of the Nasson College campus.

The Lincoln Schoolhouse in Springvale in the early 1900s. It is still a functioning school in the 1990s.

Members of the Kesslen Shoe baseball team pose for their team picture.

Indian's Last Leap is the site of a recreational picnicing and swimming spot on the Mousam River. While the romantic story of a Native American leaping to his death is probably apocraphal, this is one of the prettiest spots in Sanford.

Four
Acton, Shapleigh, Newfield, and Waterboro

Acton Corner as it appeared in the early 1900s.

An early 1900s photograph of Acton Corner with its open fields and farm scenes.

Summer and fall are traditional fair times in Maine; the Acton Fair has always been one of the most popular.

Livestock wait in anticipation at the Acton Fair, most likely for the oxen-pulling contest. Agricultural and livestock contests are still a popular part of rural fairs.

A GAR (government) camp in Acton in the 1930s.

Ossipee Lake in Waterboro Center in 1920. Between the World Wars many summer camps were built on the shores of this beautiful lake.

A 1917 postcard from Ossippe Lake of "huge fish" on the way to market. This postcard reflects the dry, wry humor of old-time Maine. While fish this size are questionable denizens of the inland York County lakes, lakes throughout the region are noted for their fine fish stocks.

A Shapleigh church, pictured
on a 1909 postcard that was
sent to Massachusetts.

Mousam Lake in Shapleigh and Acton has always been a popular summer attraction for local
people and tourists alike.

North Shapleigh in the early 1930s.

An early 1900s view of the square in North Shapleigh looking north.

The Holmes Homestead Farm in Acton, another old-time landmark. A members of the Holmes family was awarded the Congressional Medal of Honor for service to his country a century ago. Today, the farm is the home of Charles Chuck Holmes and his family.

Rural farms in West Newfield. Today Newfield is remarkably unchanged from the way it looked in the 1920s.

The Newfield Cadet Band, all dressed up for a parade and concert. Beginning with the end of the Civil War, patriotic parades and celebrations were common in rural communities. They provided excuses for people to come to town and socialize as well as reinforcing patriotism.

The bandstand in Newfield. Many concerts were held here over the years.

York County's many lakes and camps have always attracted summer visitors. This scene is of Shady Nook Camp.

The old mill and mill pond in Newfield, where the Willowbrook Village restoration has preserved much of early York County's history, heritage, and traditions. This is a worthwhile place for a day's visit with family and friends to enjoy the nostalgia and fun of rural Maine life.

The U.S. Naval Observatory with its 65-foot tower and camera as it once looked in Limerick.

A birds-eye view of Limerick Village in the early 1900s.

Dressed in their finest attire, residents cross the bridge on their way into Limerick.

A photograph of Main Street in Limerick. Note the early cars in the distance.

A wedding party poses for a family picture at the Congregational Church in Limerick.

A typical quiet summer on Main Street, Limerick.

The old Swasey Store in Limerick.

Sadler's Store, an IGA store on Main Street in Limerick, had a sign advertising convenient calling if you didn't have a phone at home yourself. Prior to the advent of large grocery chains, the IGA stores—local stores, locally owned, but supplied by a central warehouse system—were often the only grocery stores in town.

A NRA parade in Limerick, c. 1933. While Maine was staunchly Republican at the time—it was one of only two states that voted against Roosevelt in 1934—there was some support for the New Deal programs.

This cleverly altered postcard reflects some of the wry humor Maine is famous for.

Three Limerick gentlemen pose for their picture at one of the older buildings in town in this very early photograph.

The Weddel home in Limerick in the early 1900s.

A view of the Deedvan Hotel in Limerick.

Guests at a rural inn enjoy the outdoors while closed shutters keep rooms cool inside.

Early photographers often traveled to small towns and villages to take family portraits.

Horses and plows were the first step every spring to preparing the land for the year's crops.

Oxen and horses together provided the pulling power needed to bring in the crops and get them to market.

Oxen also were part of the early morning scene in rural York County as they pulled carts into town to bring goods to market.

In years past, the best way to get around during the winter in towns like Limerick was by horse and sleigh.

Yankee ingenuity often produced strange-looking but functional vehicles. This may have been the forerunner of the modern snowmobile.

Rock quarries in southern Maine provided work for residents and stone for building homes, factories, and office buildings in Maine and elsewhere in New England.

Lumber and logging provided income for many families in rural areas in years past, as they do today. Much of the forest in Limerick was totally destroyed by the forest fire of 1947. It has shown a remarkable recovery in the last fifty years.

A view of Limerick Mills from Canon Hill, taken from an old postcard published by F.C. Philpot.

Limerick Mills, and similar mills throughout southern Maine, once provided jobs for thousands of rural residents.

One-room schools like this one in Limerick were the primary system of schooling in Maine well into the twentieth century. Many people still living today will attest that the education provided by these schools and their dedicated teachers was of an extremely high quality.

Limerick Academy with its classic gazebo was a favorite meeting spot for students and residents.

Three elder citizens of Limerick at the monument for Limerick Academy.

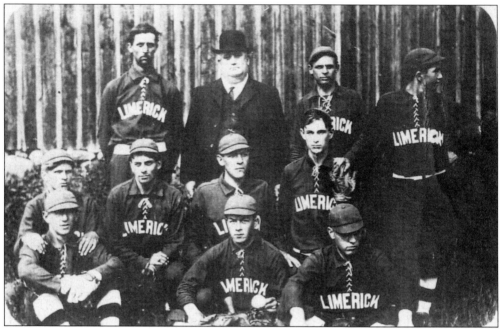

A Limerick baseball team of yesteryear proudly poses for a team photograph with their manager. Prior to World War II, almost every town in rural Maine had baseball teams. The local matches would draw large crowds to root for both teams.

The SINGING SMITH FAMILY

NOVELTY ENTERTAINERS

Limerick, Me.   R.F.D.

The renowned Singing Smith Family are shown in this early promotional postcard of the widely acclaimed "Novelty Entertainers."

Sporting events in Maine often focused on practical skills such as operating wheelbarrows.

Perhaps these are the local athletic champions about to battle it out for the title.

Unlike the majority of events today, special occasions in the past were "dress up" events, as can be seen in this old photograph.

A summer picnic in Limerick.

Five

Parsonsfield, Porter, Kezar Falls, and Cornish

An early postcard of a church in Parsonsfield, the northernmost town in York County.

From Limerick, the foothills of the White Mountains begin to rise up. This photograph, taken from a hill, shows the rolling hills and farmlands of East Parsonsfield.

Drake's Corner Waterfall in Parsonsfield, with the old mill as it looked in the early 1900s.

General stores were the the centers of rural Maine communities. Parsonsfield, a large town which rises from the Ossipee River into the hills, has numerous small stores to this day.

A photograph of Orchard Grange, which was one of the key gathering spots for rural and farm families when granges were major community organizations in rural areas across America. Originally started as a political lobbying effort at the time of the Greenback Party, it eventually became a social and fraternal organization.

A street scene in East Parsonsfield.

A tree-lined street in East Parsonsfield.

Charles Dearborn's house in front of Fenderson's Store in East Parsonsfield, with a well and bucket in the foreground.

The post office at East Parsonsfield, as the first cars made their way into rural York County.

The view entering West Parsonsfield as two residents stroll down the lane with their pet cat. Nearby, the winter's supply of wood to heat their homes stands cut, stacked, and ready.

An early scenic postcard of Old Church Hill, with its winding road and rocky pastures.

One of Parsonsfield's early churches.

The Parsonsfield Seminary c. 1900.

Parsonsfield Seminary was an early religious training and learning center for surrounding communities.

An artist's rendition of Parsonsfield Seminary in the 1900s.

The Reading Room in Parsonsfield Seminary.

A turn-of-the-century photograph of North Parsonsfield.

A view of North Parsonsfield, with Green Mountain in the background.

The Free Baptist Church in South Parsonsfield.

Children in rural Maine always enjoyed their wooden wagons as this boy does near his home in South Parsonsfield. If he seems to be frowning, you can understand why: the pile of wood still needs to be moved.

The Old Faithful covered bridge connecting Parsonsfield and Porter. It still stands as a delightful historic landmark today.

Indian Glen, a popular rest and watering spot in Porter in the good old days.

An early view of Main Street in Porter.

Freedom Street in Porter, with a sign that directs travelers to North Parsonsfield, only 1 mile distant.

One of the oldest known pictures of Porter's first post office.

A charming view of Spectacle Pond in Kezar Falls.

A classic winter scene of North Main Street in Kezar Falls.

The W.T. Norton store, a source for grains and groceries in Kezar Falls.

Bridge Street in Kezar Falls as it looked in the early 1900s.

A later view of Bridge Street in Kezar Falls.

The Kezar Falls Post Office, c. 1900.

A view of the bank and post office block in Kezar Falls from what may have been a promotional postcard of the 1930s.

A turn-of-the-century photograph of Pilsbury House in Kezar Falls.

An elegant home is graced by a white picket fence in this scene from Kezar Falls.

The grand Malvern Hotel, a Kezar Falls landmark, as it looked for many years.

M. E. Church, KEZAR FALLS, Maine.
Rev. Cymbrid Hughes, Pastor.

An early postcard of the Methodist Epsipocal Church and its pastor, Reverend Cymbrid Hughes.

Kezar Falls Woolen Mills, with a mother and her daugher in the fashionable transportation of the day.

The early Kezar Falls High School. The children of Kezar Falls now attend the regional Saccopee Valley High School.

The Blue Stockings, a winning 1908 baseball team that earned fame in its day for Kezar Falls.

An early postcard of the bridge in Kezar Falls.

The new bridge at Kezar Falls may be more durable, but it is not as attractive as the one it replaced.

Middle Dam, Kezar Falls, as depicted in a c. 1900s postcard.

A grand view of Cornish from Towle's Hill.

High Street in Cornish, with its hitching posts, picket fences, and graceful trees that gave the town its rural charm.

A view of Main Street in Cornish during winter. At times like this, horse-drawn sleighs replaced carriages for shopping trips from farm to town.

Maple Street in Cornish.

The Ira Garland Clothing Store in Cornish featured clothing and styles of the early 1900s. Note the sign—cash store!

Chipman's Drugstore, as it looked in years gone by. Notice that they served sodas, sundaes, and frappes, and featured Hood's Ice Cream; a name that is still around today.

The Lincoln in Cornish, one of the grand old country homes favored by early vacationers in Maine.

The New Lincoln Hotel, which replaced the original landmark hotel when it was lost in a fire.

For many years, horses provided the basic transportation for residents of rural Maine. The Chaplin horseshoe barn was the spot in Cornish to be sure your horses were well shod.

Waiting for friends and vistors at the Cornish station when the railroads were the popular and easy way to travel in rural Maine.

An early photograph of the old school building in Cornish.

Students from various grades of the Cornish school gathered for this photograph after classes were done for the day.

124

Children's summer camps were one of rural Maine's early business success stories. Here, counselors and campers take part in a flag-lowering ceremony at the end of the camping day.

Water sports, canoeing, and rowing among them, were popular pastimes at camps in rural York County and throughout Maine.

Cornish was always known for its enjoyable parades, which included many residents of town. Dick Dyer is identified as one of the parade spectators pictured here.

Company M of the Maine National Guard stands for inspection before the traditional Fourth of July parade in 1907.

Early photographs were often developed as postcards so people could send pictures of themselves and their family to friends.

In this parade float you can easily identify Maude Gilpatrick, Ima Small, Josie Perry, Mrs. Taylor, Lina Knight, George Perry, and James Taylor.

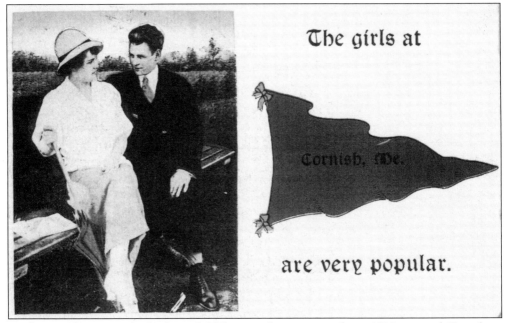

The girls at

Cornish, Me.

are very popular.

"Girls Are Always Popular In Cornish." That was the saying on this c. 1900 postcard. But, if you visited other towns, you just might see the same card with that town's name.

Acknowledgments

We gratefully acknowledge the help and advice we have received from many knowledgeable old-time Mainers who trace their family roots back for generations. To Nancy Hooper, Connie Porter Scott, Charles Holmes, Louise Russell, Harlan Taylor, Georgia Perry, Glen Garrish, plus the many families pictured and mentioned in this book, we express our appreciation.

Without the special help and thoughtfulness of postcard collector Rick Poore, this book could not have captured the wide range of old-time photographs that portray many of the historic buildings, activities, and traditions that were part of rural York County.

Many astute librarians, local historians, and history buffs also provided suggestions and sources for photographs. The result of all these efforts has enabled us to provide what we hope is an enjoyable trip into history of early rural Maine.

We also acknowledge the useful historic insights from the 1832 Edition of William D. Williamson's *History of Maine*. We trust that you'll find this unique perspective of early Maine history fascinating as it recounts the roots of rural York County's towns and villages.